The Thrilling Sources of Push the Envelope
and Other Idioms

by Arnold Ringstad • illustrated by Dan McGeehan

Published by The Child's World®
1980 Lookout Drive • Mankato, MN 56003-1705
800-599-READ • www.childsworld.com

Acknowledgments
The Child's World®: Mary Berendes, Publishing Director
The Design Lab: Design and production
Red Line Editorial: Editorial direction

Design elements: Kirsty Pargeter/iStockphoto

ISBN 9781614732372
LCCN 2012932814

Printed in the United States of America
Mankato, MN
July 2012
PA02118

Contents

RAT RACE

MEANING: A **rat race** is an endless, pointless pursuit.

ORIGIN: This phrase comes from the way rats run in a wheel or through a maze.

EXAMPLE: When Chloe's father left for work, he joked that he was off to the **rat race**.

THERE'S THE RUB

MEANING: When a person says "**there's the rub**," they mean "there's the difficulty."

ORIGIN: This phrase refers to an old sport played outdoors. An uneven area in the grass that made a ball bounce strangely was called a *rub*. The phrase was first used by William Shakespeare in his play *Hamlet*.

EXAMPLE: "**There's the rub**," Logan said. "We can't play a real basketball game with only three people."

RUN-OF-THE-MILL

MEANING: Something that is **run-of-the-mill** is the ordinary, basic version of something.

ORIGIN: This idiom comes from mills that wove clothing. Items that came directly from the mill were cheap and basic.

EXAMPLE: Some of Luis' classmates used fancy mechanical pencils. He preferred to use a **run-of-the-mill** wooden one.

HOT OFF THE PRESSES

MEANING: Something that is **hot off the presses** is freshly printed.

ORIGIN: This phrase comes from an old way of printing. This process used hot metal. Later, it came to mean anything freshly printed.

EXAMPLE: Bianca got the newspaper **hot off the presses** to read the student council election results.

NOSE TO THE GRINDSTONE

MEANING: When you put your **nose to the grindstone**, you work especially hard.

ORIGIN: The origin of this idiom is uncertain. It may come from the process of sharpening knives on a stone called a grindstone. The person doing it would have to get their face very close to the grindstone.

EXAMPLE: Wesley always put his **nose to the grindstone** on the night before a big test.

PUSH THE ENVELOPE

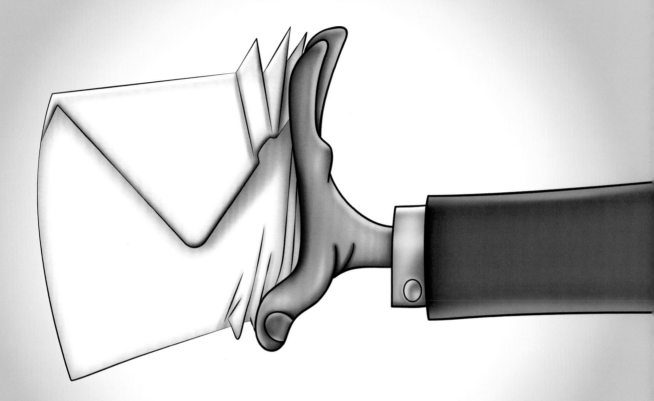

MEANING: When you **push the envelope**, you try to go beyond the limits of performance.

ORIGIN: This phrase comes from airplanes and flying. The word *envelope* is used as a math term. It describes the limits of an airplane's performance.

EXAMPLE: Javier read about astronauts who **pushed the envelope** of space travel.

JACK-OF-ALL-TRADES

MEANING: A **Jack-of-all-trades** is a person who is good at many things.

ORIGIN: The name *Jack* has been used in English to mean a common man. It doesn't refer to a particular person named Jack.

EXAMPLE: Cole was a **Jack-of-all-trades**. He was great at math, a skilled athlete, and a strong reader.

KEEP ONE'S CARDS CLOSE TO ONE'S CHEST

MEANING: If you **keep your cards close to your chest**, you are careful not to give away your strategy.

ORIGIN: This phrase comes from card games in which you don't want the other players to see your cards. If you hold the cards close to your chest, it prevents others from seeing them.

EXAMPLE: Audrey was planning her mom's surprise party, so she had to **keep her cards close to her chest.**

JURY-RIGGED

MEANING: A thing that is fixed by patching parts together is **jury-rigged**.

ORIGIN: This phrase has been used since at least the 1600s to describe a ship's mast that has been patched together. It is uncertain where it originally came from.

EXAMPLE: Gavin's broken glasses were **jury-rigged** together with tape.

BE THERE OR BE SQUARE

MEANING: When someone says "**be there or be square**," they mean "be there or be unpopular."

ORIGIN: This phrase refers to a meaning of the word *square* that started in the 1930s in the United States. The word meant old-fashioned or not exciting.

EXAMPLE: When Alejandro invited people to his party, he always joked, "**Be there or be square!**"

NOT IN KANSAS ANYMORE

MEANING: When you are no longer in comfortable, familiar surroundings, you are **not in Kansas anymore**.

ORIGIN: This phrase comes from the 1939 film *The Wizard of Oz*. The character Dorothy says it after she is transported to another land.

EXAMPLE: When Erika stepped off the airplane in Germany, she turned to her sister and said, "We're **not in Kansas anymore**."

HOT POTATO

MEANING: A **hot potato** is a controversial issue that is risky to talk about, especially in politics.

ORIGIN: This idiom comes from the fact that potatoes stay hot for a long time. If you hold onto a hot potato too long, you might get burned.

EXAMPLE: The issue of removing chocolate milk from the lunchroom was a **hot potato** at student council meetings.

SMELL A RAT

MEANING: If you **smell a rat**, you suspect something is wrong.

ORIGIN: This phrase may have come from when rats were commonly found in homes. Dogs hunted them. If a dog smelled a rat, there was something wrong.

EXAMPLE: Jenna's brothers insisted they didn't eat the last cookie, but she could **smell a rat**.

BORN WITH A SILVER SPOON IN ONE'S MOUTH

MEANING: If you are **born with a silver spoon in your mouth**, you are born into a wealthy family.

ORIGIN: This phrase may have come from a tradition in wealthy families of giving children silver spoons. It also may simply refer to the fact that the rich used silver spoons instead of wooden ones.

EXAMPLE: Jada was **born with a silver spoon in her mouth**. Her father was a doctor and her mother a banker.

WATCH MY SIX

MEANING: When someone says "**watch my six**," they mean "watch out behind me."

ORIGIN: This phrase comes from fighter pilots. They refer to positions as numbers on a clock. Twelve o'clock would be directly ahead and six o'clock would be directly behind.

EXAMPLE: Quentin asked his friends to **watch his six** when he walked into the haunted house.

BEAT AROUND THE BUSH

MEANING: If you **beat around the bush**, you avoid talking about the main point.

ORIGIN: This phrase comes from bird hunting. Some people would beat a bush, and others would use nets to catch the birds that flew out.

EXAMPLE: Diana didn't know the answer to her friend's question, so she **beat around the bush**.

IT'S ALL GREEK TO ME

MEANING: If you can't read or understand something, **it's all Greek to you.**

ORIGIN: This phrase suggests that anything you can't read might as well be written in Greek. It was used in William Shakespeare's *Julius Caesar*, but it originally comes from a Latin proverb.

EXAMPLE: Fifth-grader Ricky tried to read a college engineering textbook, but **it was all Greek to him**.

THROW SOMEONE A CURVEBALL

MEANING: If you **throw someone a curveball**, you surprise him or her with something that is difficult to deal with.

ORIGIN: This idiom comes from the sport of baseball. A curveball is a kind of pitch that is difficult to hit.

EXAMPLE: Casey **threw Natasha a curveball** when she said she could not work on their group project that evening.

SAWBUCK

MEANING: A **sawbuck** is a ten-dollar bill.

ORIGIN: US currency used to have roman numerals on it, so the ten-dollar bill had an X. This reminded people of an old-fashioned sawhorse, which was also called a sawbuck.

EXAMPLE: Damian thought it was getting harder and harder to get a nice dinner for less than a **sawbuck**.

WET YOUR WHISTLE

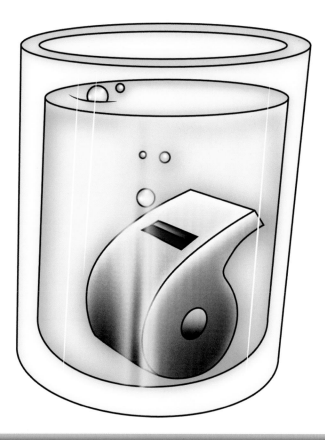

MEANING: When you **wet your whistle**, you take a drink.

ORIGIN: In the past, the mouth was sometimes referred to as a whistle. It was especially used in connection with singing or whistling. It is also difficult to sing or whistle with a dry mouth.

EXAMPLE: Reginald liked to **wet his whistle** with a cool glass of water before he sang for people.

YAHOO

MEANING: A **yahoo** is a loud, foolish, violent person.

ORIGIN: The term comes from Jonathan Swift's 1726 novel *Gulliver's Travels*. In the book, Yahoos were savage and cowardly characters.

EXAMPLE: Gina disliked it when the other basketball team's fans acted like **yahoos**.

NEW YORK MINUTE

MEANING: A **New York minute** is a very short amount of time.

ORIGIN: This phrase refers to the fast pace of life in New York City. It was probably coined by people from elsewhere in the United States.

EXAMPLE: When Mr. Silverman brought donuts to class, they were always gone in a **New York minute**.

DEUS EX MACHINA

GET OUT OF TROUBLE FREE!

MEANING: A **deus ex machina** (DAY-oos eks MA-keen-ah) is a quick way to solve a plot problem in a story, even if it doesn't make sense.

ORIGIN: This phrase is Latin for "god from the machine." It comes from Greek and Roman plays, where a plot problem was often fixed by having a god solve it.

EXAMPLE: Morgan enjoyed the movie until the end. The director just used a **deus ex machina** to resolve the story.

JUMP THE GUN

MEANING: If you **jump the gun**, you do something before the appropriate time.

ORIGIN: This idiom comes from the practice of using a pistol shot to start a race.

EXAMPLE: Dante had to be careful not to **jump the gun** and start playing his violin solo early.

NO-BRAINER

MEANING: Something that is a **no-brainer** is an easy decision.

ORIGIN: This term suggests that a decision is so easy you don't need to use your brain. It was first used in this way in a Canadian newspaper in the 1960s.

EXAMPLE: Elizabeth's friends had a hard time deciding between chocolate chip or oatmeal raisin cookies. For Elizabeth it was a **no-brainer**.

RUBBERNECKING

MEANING: A person who twists their neck to see something is **rubbernecking**.

ORIGIN: The twisting and stretching of a person's neck is compared to the stretching of rubber. The phrase was originally used by people living in large cities. They would use it to make fun of visitors from the country who would look up at tall buildings.

EXAMPLE: When Rodney went to New York City, he couldn't stop **rubbernecking** in Times Square.

SOUPED UP

MEANING: When you **soup up** something, you make it more powerful.

ORIGIN: This idiom was originally used to describe cars. It likely combined *supercharger*, a device to make cars go faster, with *soup*, a drug given to horses to make them run faster.

EXAMPLE: Gloria **souped up** her computer by adding bigger speakers and more memory.

LOOSE CANNON

MEANING: A **loose cannon** is a person or thing that is difficult to control.

ORIGIN: This phrase comes from cannons used on sailing ships. If they got loose, they could roll around the deck of the ship dangerously.

EXAMPLE: Cynthia was a **loose cannon** on the basketball court because she often dropped the ball.

About the Author

Arnold Ringstad lives in Minneapolis, where he graduated from the University of Minnesota in 2011. He enjoys reading books about space exploration and playing board games with his girlfriend. Writing about idioms makes him as happy as a clam.

About the Illustrator

Dan McGeehan loves being an illustrator. His art appears in many magazines and children's books. He currently lives in Oklahoma.